Secret Poets

Darren Donohue

Secret Poets

First published 2022

Turas Press

6-9 Trinity Street

Dublin D02 EY47

Ireland.

info@turaspress.ie

www.turaspress.ie

Copyright © 2022 Darren Donohue

The author asserts his moral rights in accordance with the provisions of the Copyright and Related acts, 2000.

All rights reserved. The contents of this publication are protected by copyright law, except as may be permitted by law, no part of the material may be reproduced (including by storage in a retrieval system) or transmitted in any form or by any means; adapted; rented or lent without the written permission of the copyright owner.

British Library Cataloguing: Data A CIP catalogue record for this book is available from the British Library.

ISBN print edition: 978-1-913598-30-3

ISBN EPub: 978-1-913598-35-8

ISBN MOBI: 978-1-913598-31-0

Cover design by Angie Crowe

Cover image by Steve Neville

Interior typesetting by Printwell Design, Dublin 3

Printed in Ireland by SPRINTprint

for Margaret, Emily, and Mary

Contents

Late at Night 7
Woke 8
Good Advice 9
Crocodile 11
Sunday Bath 13
Re-enactment 15
Sister 16
Eight Cows Electrocuted by Fallen Power Cable 17
Postcard 18
Sanctuary 19
The Riddle of Du Fu's Aunt 20
The Weed 21
Selfie 22
Bicycle 23
Curragh of Kildare 25
Your Swinging Gates 26
Ryan's Field 27
The Married Men of Stand House Road 28
Katydid 29
Magician 30
Venus in Kilmuckridge 31
Escape Hatch 32
Refugee 33
Betrayal 34
Every Little Lie 35
Gate 36
Kitchen 37
Wanderlust 38

Home School 39
Following the News 40
The Bank Clerk 41
Rehearsals 42
Respite 44
Celebration 45
Caving at Kilcorney 46
Play Date 47
Secret Poets 48
The Beacon 49
Lost & Found 51
Prayer 52
Emily 53
Lohan 54
I Found the Words 55
The Singing Scab 57
The Tuesday I spied a man discovering his soul 58
Graveyard Mass 59
Casting Off 60
Musical Chairs 61
Crossing 62
After Surgery 63
The Hare 64
The Crucified Christ 65
Grace 66
The Bell-Ringers 67
A Still Life 68

Acknowledgements 71
About the Author 73

Late at Night

Late at night,
when the moon rolls on its side,
and empty fields mourn history,
dictators kill poets.

Surprised in their pyjamas,
stolen from their beds,
they're marched to where firing squads
miss their target,
taking one, two, three bullets
to send geckos flying
in the hidden dark.

A wooden-legged school teacher
and two anarchist matadors
are trapped like paper
between scissor-blade headlights.

Lorca, standing apart,
dips his pen in their shadows
and draws their faces
in rings of gun smoke.

The briefest silence
and petty rage
whistles through him,
dragging the poet
from his balcony of stars
into an unmarked grave.

Woke

It was as though I woke up inside a riot—smoke, gunshots, screams.
I couldn't see the sky or tell if it was night or day.

*

It was as though we were swept off our feet by outrage and blown down frantic streets. Missiles flew, trailing sequins like destroying stars and, for an instant, our darkness gleamed.

*

It was as though the city trembled, afraid to know itself. Artificial lakes forgot their purpose, tower blocks threw down their shadows, surprised statues buckled at the knee or clung to their marble plinths.

*

It was as though we were the sickness and the cure, a purging righteousness slicing through brick, glass and steel to find the city's naked heart. It was as though time crumbled while circling its walls, waiting for the killing to stop.

Good Advice

I hung on his every word,
after all, he was the youngest of 21 children
and had 82% of his body tattooed.
Adding these figures together, I quickly concluded
this stranger was 103 times wiser than me.

First off, he listed his ailments.
They were many.
How had he coped with these afflictions?
With simple good grace.
Next came his time in prison,
years spent between his cell, the workshop
and the yard. Those 'boys' were his brothers,
he missed them, missed the solidarity of incarceration.
Then came love. 'Never mind them,' he said.
'They don't understand us, will never understand us.
What they want and we can give will never meet.'
This led to his child, his only child,
his son, his pride and joy. 'He's in college,' he said.
'He's on the right road, he'll make something of himself.'

All of a sudden, I felt the cold. All of a sudden,
this train journey turned a bend. His stop was fast approaching,
Athy, its detox clinic. He had only a half-bottle
of wine left. Things turned serious. He told me I had
a demon on my shoulder, he could see it. He said,
someone called Jason meant me harm. I stayed quiet,
people were uncomfortable.

Athy was announced over the intercom and I suggested
he get his things together. He suggested,
I mind my own business. I reminded him of his appointment
and talked of his son as I walked his bag slowly
toward the train door. He followed me to the exit,
the great horror awaiting him the other side.

As we parted, he gave me his venom. In a single moment,
all I'd been given—
the love, the opportunity, the high-minded ideals—
stood between us like a peacock. The colours blinded him
as he stepped from the train into the waiting arms of good advice.

I returned to my seat and looked out the window.
A plane flew through the sky as the train
pulled out of the station.

Crocodile

Languidly, a crocodile stretches across
the hospital waiting room floor. Its mouth

slightly ajar, exposing a war chest of shadow teeth.
I shift uneasily on my hard plastic seat.

Despite all the weight I've lost, it still manages
a groan. Scattered about, others also consider

the crocodile, or cradle their phones, or dream
with their eyes open. They all expect bad news.

Perhaps, we can pool our sorrow and lay it
at the feet of Jeanne Hebuterne

as she walks through snow, her hands pressed
to the soft crown of her unborn child.

Arriving at Saint-Etienne morgue,
they led her down endless corridors

to find Modigliani frozen.
She cut a lock of her hair. I watch her weave it

through his fingers and bind them
tight as a promise. The following morning,

she rose from her bed and threw herself
from the fifth-floor balcony. A crowd

circled around her, forming the walls of a well,
allowing her to sink through cracks in the pavement.

She floats across these hospital walls, painted battleship grey,
pinned with posters living with cancer.

Her tears are perfectly preserved in watercoolers,
they wait around every corner, eager to console us.

Doors bark and wail, and my name is announced,
the crocodile grins and whips its tail.

Sunday Bath

The surface of the Earth is 71% water.

An angry torrent storms the bathtub,
some adult hand swims back and forth across
the perfect sheet paper surface,
splashing about like a hooked fish.

I'm dropped like a lobster into a scalding pot,
my arms flailing against the tub's rigid indifference.
I hold my breath and plunge beneath the waves.
My chicken liver lungs kick against muscle and bone,
my heart slows to a steady thump.

Bits of sky and prophecy snag on the plughole
or drift by like deep-sea fish. Caked with soap,
muffled voices sing a sirens' chorus, bittersweet and insistent.
Bubbles, like prayers, surround me,
delicate and practical as a dream.
Somewhere between sinking and floating,
I come to a stop, resting my head on a creel of eels.

Noah's flood lasted one year and ten days.

I sit my child in the bath and water builds up
around her. With a hand pressed to the tap,
she intently watches it rise. I check the temperature
every two seconds, as though I could protect her
from the swell lifting her like a pebble

and crowding the vacant space about her. Evening withdraws
shyly through the window, letting us be for now,
taking a final look over its shoulder
before stretching deep shadows across every garden
and painting a solemn moon into every puddle.

Re-enactment

Erecting a great guillotine on my lawn, they woke me from my sleep. From the window, I watched them exchange t-shirts and shorts for uniforms with dark insignias and tinfoil medals. A chorus of school children marched up the driveway, singing rebel songs and carrying banners commemorating 1922. To deafening applause, stopping at my washing line, they hung out Irish flags along its entire length. A truck arrived and began distributing replica weaponry – rifles, old muskets, hand grenades. More people arrived – men, women, children, and they began digging deep trenches either side of my greenhouse. There was a sound like thunder as a fleet of Chinese tanks rolled into position, flattening my orchids. Still more people came – nurses, doctors, bishops, pensioners, all carrying a gun or waving flags. My window pane rattled as a Russian bomber circled overhead. At some invisible cue, everyone suddenly withdrew into their assigned company. They sectioned off my garden, establishing barbed wire fences and checkpoints. All trained their weapons on the other and, once the building work ceased, a terrible silence settled. A tall man, wearing a uniform I didn't recognise, entered my bedroom unannounced. He asked if I wanted to be a soldier, a prisoner, or a refugee? I couldn't think what to answer and simply gestured toward my garden. The man smiled and said, in the end it would make little difference, I'd still help to feed the ovens.

Sister

I slept outside your bedroom,
stretched out like a sphinx on the old carpet.
I was afraid to wake you,
yet needed an inch of your clean edge.

There was a music box among your things.
When you pinched the clasp
as though unbuttoning your blouse,
a leaning darkness slipped away.

Each morning your mirror was clouded,
cut with shards of mist. It never wasted
an opportunity to champion loneliness
or fetch from some hidden drawer

square pictures dusted with age. At night the corners
would buckle and retreat into memory,
unable to offer you anything
beyond what you could see.

Eight Cows Electrocuted by Fallen Power Cable

Eight beautiful Clare cows are electrocuted in a windy field
Eight wondrous cows
Who – born elsewhere –
Would have been adored
Worshipped

Eight miraculous planets
Orbiting haystacks and a barren red barn
Constant as sorrow
Unknowable as rain
Unreachable as faith

Eight marvellous cows standing on legs of iron
Flat packed
Large sad eyes forgiving everyone everything
Floating slowly across rolled-out fields
My breath catches when I see you
Nature's lawnmowers
The space between you always perfect

Dear gentle spirits, who knew only peace
Who never doubted the field's narrow dimensions
Who watched each morning-skin-night
What did God know to strike you down
His arbitrary love arrived with a blackout
Ten thousand homes plunged into darkness
Only your soft eyes flared

Postcard

Can the church bells of Nice heal me?
I stand by her castle gates, deciphering
patterns in the sea. They creep forward,
tumbling over the lightest blue.

A holy procession appears from an alley,
the priest four-cornered beneath a red canopy.
He's singing with the faithful,
their hymn washing over the cobblestones,
children throw rose petals to sweeten the air,
their parents moving in step, clutching their bibles.
But before I can ask for the right prayer,
they vanish through a glowering arch.

With eyes shut, I swim out between corridors
of melting waves. Hungry for release,
clawing the shore, they spin me around
like the hand on a compass.

Sanctuary

Waking in my cot to silence and darkness,
both determined, as illness, to humble.
Nothing stirs. Midnight stillness holds its breath.

I won't cry out, not me, even then.
The room reveals itself in that blue light
snow masters, aglow on farmyard gates

or pulsing between chimney stacks.
There are others here cooing in their sleep,
wrapped up in worlds I can't imagine.

I peep through the cot's slim bars and,
inch by inch, vast outlines shimmer
and harden, valleys and mountain peaks

steeped in winter fog. I raise my hands
and study their tiny grasp, little fingers
learning to hold a million nameless things.

I'll climb from this new womb
and seek out my old sanctuary. There,
planted in the soil of human contact,

my translucent eyelids will thicken
and vines secure my budding heart,
like laces through a boot.

The Riddle of Du Fu's Aunt

While plague swept through China, a travelling sorceress visited Du Fu's Aunt. Du Fu's mother had died following his birth and he was raised by her sister. She had a child of the same age and the two toddlers shared a room. The sorceress observed all this and prophesied, the child who slept by the window would survive the plague. The story claims, the Aunt lifted her baby out of his cot by the window and placed Du Fu in his bed. The plague took her son and Du Fu survived, but he was to always live under the shadow of this great sacrifice.

And so, the riddle was born: why did she save Du Fu at the expense of her own son?

Please allow me to set the record straight, freeing Du Fu from this ridiculous burden and ironing out this wrinkle in his biographical history.

Being a practical woman, Du Fu's Aunt placed both toddlers in the cot by the window. But only Du Fu pulled himself up, morning and evening, to marvel at the sun's rise and fall.

The Weed

What must the weed make of it all?
After a lifetime of pushing, growing,
stretching, flowering, to find itself
embedded between two concrete walls,
its feet planted in some mother crack,
the little chink through which it sprang.

The view— a grey concrete garden competing
with a heavy grey sky, a modest peach house
with matching drains, a mossy chimney stack
black with soot, old bits of pipe drooling
over an outhouse roof, a shy breeze now
and then. How absurd! And yet, the weed
continues its journey upward, trying to see

over the wall and into the next garden.
What patience! Such perseverance!
Teach me, little weed, your inexhaustible curiosity,
your blind faith, your undiminished character
and infinite certainty. Look on me and share
the allegiance to which your root is tapped.

Selfie

Obsessed with the selfie was Philip Larkin.
He'd set the timer, run and jump in
to pose with a newspaper, or sorting his books,
his posture as neatly arranged as his looks.

There's one where he scowls out a window,
his face the very picture of a grieving widower.
In another, he stares down the lens directly,
glaring at the camera and frowning intensely.

There's something of the actor preparing his role,
piecing together bits of characters he stole.
Or vanity demanding to be taken seriously—
the clown and his tears, expecting pity.

I imagine the action after the snap,
when he corks the camera and lies down for a nap.
His hair tossed, his fabled glasses gone,
a slight smile as though he remembers a song.

All pretence stripped away,
carefree, as a boy off school for the day.
It's from this place his poetry came,
to shred his portrait, to smash the frame.

Bicycle

My bicycle delivers me—
through a sleepy village,
moving at last
at the speed that I think—
to the river.

A swan nests on her island.
She swims over
to show me her prehistoric feet.
They weave motion,
opening and closing
like dark cabbage leaves.

Through its arched eyes
the bridge extends a view—
reflecting and continuing.
Everything is silent and still,
held so completely in place
I look for the frame
enclosing this canvas.

A fish jumps,
and jumps again.
I see it break water,
pointing skyward like a silver finger.
Its landing uncoils rings
that move slowly over the water.
Does he know,

down among his dark reeds,
the impression he has left
echoing across the river?
Ripples linger,
inching further
and further
from the centre.

I jump back on my bicycle
and peddle back to when I was
part swan, part bridge, part fish.

Curragh of Kildare

My childhood playground,
open sky landscape, sweeping
east to west. Secret scrub corridors
for hunters of chance, for pinching

sap from nature's crown.
The military graveyard – hip hillock fixed,
we climb the camel's back
to rest beneath a thinly drawn elm.

Heroes of WWI sleep, quilt turf covered.
Cracked tombstones sigh:
We are but ships on a freezing wave,
sinking now, ground deep. Child cloud-blown

downhill, coming to rest in Donnelly's Hollow
between pools of shadow-cold. Motherless dark,
creeping giants of fortune, my Curragh reflects
your wide wind-sweep and relentless swallow.

Your Swinging Gates

I shoulder your coffin and walk from the church.
Those you touched, loved, scared – fall in behind.

My father spoke often of the river men and their dark ways.
How, late at night, they drifted slowly by your cottage.
A young widow with three small children, back bent,
trying to cut a life from the bog. I knew you only
by the stove, hands folded neatly in your lap.

We gain the graveyard and the breach waits.
'Waits for all,' it yawns, mouth-wide with darkness.
Your coffin drops with a dull thud, the sound of my head
hitting the pillow. I take refuge by the damp clay,
heaped up, hungry to heal the wound. When I reach back
for you now, the first thing I touch are your swinging gates.

They were painted black and white and opened onto the road.
I'd wrap myself around them, kick out and fly through the air.
Then the sudden stop and fling back,
like time reversed, or memory predicting the future.
Everything in motion, dancing toward me and spinning away,
the canal dipping in and out of view.

Ryan's Field

She dangles her bag of carrots,
eager to feed the donkey.
He seeks her out with his large eyes,

craning his neck over a metal gate.
We cycled to this place, a lumpy field
enclosed by flowering hedgerows.

It's our daily pilgrimage, skirting potholes,
to embrace this simple act of giving. He accepts
the offering with delight, complete as a circle.

On tiptoes, she strokes his wide forehead.
Her song races across the fields
to climb the church steeple and wake the bell.

The Married Men of Stand House Road

On sunny days, they take their lawnmowers
for a walk. At the weekend, they flirt

with the off-licence. When together, they lean
forward as though around a campfire.

At home, they lean back and stroke a tiny
plastic box. At night, they sit up late,

shuffling bills like a deck of cards. They dream,
but say they never remember their dreams.

They're first to rise on Monday mornings
and stand dazed beneath a watering can.

They spit-shine their cars on Sunday afternoons
and drive their miniatures to a museum

for the old. If you greet them, they sew their hands
to their hips and turn like weathervanes.

Katydid

Little leaf bug,
you've risen imitation
to impossible heights,
transforming it
into a new identity.

Only vigilant watchers
will catch you out.
Six web-spun legs,
two hair-thin antennae,
no discernible eyes,
and the revelation
of your emerald costume.

At night, you feast
on your double,
singing a rough chorus.
My perfect cannibal.

You've even mastered
the essence of decay,
your careful mask
almost mocking
a leaf's passing.

When I see you,
your back burnt through
with spots of autumn brown,
I'm forced to conclude
your great study transcends
your humble subject.

Magician

Somewhere a mower chomps grass,
humming away to itself,
we work to prune the pear trees.

Quietly they sprouted a slim-fingered
canopy with tips erupting and birthing
flower. A dry satisfying snap and branches

are cut free. I toss them to your rake,
combing the soft lawn, the fallen
gathered into neat piles. On my ladder

the fields unlock, the view jumping
boundary walls and sprinting toward
the mountain. I watch myself as one would

a strange magician, his act—
the miraculous feat of shaping nature,
stunting growth in order to encourage it.

You hum along with the mower,
your song, a melody of honest endeavour
this great bounty winked into existence.

Venus in Kilmuckridge

I take off along the rippling edge,
a hard sand cold against my feet.

Diffused light cancels any trace
of the horizon, seamlessly stitching the sea

and sky into a single tapestry. Fishing boats
float like hot air balloons, and buoys

hover uncertainly among the clouds.
How far will my body carry me,

skipping through thin veils of ocean spray?
Up ahead, storm petrels are perfecting

their signatures, twisting and dipping.
The swell rings in my ears, raging,

and then suddenly quiet, fickle as Venus,
bathed in blue, casually fingering the sprawl.

Escape Hatch

Matisse and I share a complaint,
a debilitating disease of the stomach.
His was born out of anxiety.
Like most young men,
he only knew what he *didn't* want to do.
He didn't want to run the family business
(much to his father's annoyance);
he didn't want to become a lawyer
(his father's sense of second best).
And so, he fell ill, taking to the bed
with paralysing stomach cramps.

The days were endless,
as he only rose to trek from his bed
to the bathroom. Matisse and I
share this prolonged exile to a country
where patience becomes currency,
where the will fights, flees,
and eventually surrenders,
to the brutal reality of physical pain. One day,
his mother came to him carrying a box.
She saw her son wasting away,
unable to turn over, barely able to open his eyes.
She left the box by his side, calling it 'a distraction'.
Matisse reached for her paint box,
he lifted the latch and, yearning to escape,
he leapt through the hatch.

Refugee

She appeared from the darkness
stepping carefully into curving
yellow light. Behind her, a wild night—

starless, freezing hail, bitter gales.
Surprised in our little home, sitting before
an ancient fire, we turned to find her feral gaze

resting on us, her breath frosting patio glass.
What did you see, little cat? Your face eaten
by battles fought in a strange landscape.

The children rushed to your aid, splashing
milk into plastic bowls. Swinging wide
the doors they found only a storm where

you'd stood. Beyond our yellowing rim
the wind howled, the stars refused
to shine, the freezing hail bared its teeth.

Betrayal

You were convinced *The Taking of Christ* was a fake.
An obvious copy painted by someone/somewhere/somewhen,
an impressive counterfeit masquerading
as a masterpiece. You'd studied Art History,
your knowledge hard-won and cherished.
You were amused by everyone's devotion
to what was clearly a forgery.

Many afternoons we sat before it, you
pointing out the flaws in the composition. Your visceral
insight elevated language, verb and noun,
dragging them uphill like boulders. I sat by your side,
watching the scene unfold—
the soldiers, their armour, that kiss.

One wet Tuesday, I visited the canvas alone,
drawn by the suspicion I was a pale imitation,
a thin portrait sketched by another.
A sudden impulse compelled me to reach out
and touch the painting. Did I imagine Judas,
his eyes wide with dark delight,
slyly incline his head toward me and wink?

Every Little Lie

She smoked *Sweet Afton*
and wore whiskers like a walrus. She died
sitting up, a wedding album open in her lap.

She called me Sonny.

Each morning I sat quietly on her bed
watching her dress. Her body,
smooth and round as a globe.
I often curled up there, pushing my sins
into her staying hand, the world shrinking
to accommodate my first crop of gratitude,
carefully harvested, almost without knowing.

I called her Anna Mae.

Each night she knelt by my bedside
blowing wild stories into my ear.
Every little lie, a slate in the roof of memory.
Every word scouting ahead,
clearing a path through the long grass.

Then the terrible moving away,
then an ever shortening wedge of light,
then the squeak and roar of darkness.

Gate

You're collapsed at an angle,
as though tilting your head

to consider black lines drawn
through freshly cut fields. In rain,

you cower like a frightened animal,
dipping your rusty muzzle in puddles

to sup like cattle. On sunny days,
there's all this talk of having you replaced,

measurements are taken and you're banged
and shuck. But on early mornings, veiled in mist,

you appear naked as an open heart,
each rectangular chamber

framing an intimate portrait,
nature boundless, longing for fulfilment.

Kitchen

The kettle is a dominatrix,
watching me with one steaming eye,

demanding coffee with sugar and a splash of milk.
The kitchen table died standing on its spindly legs.

Strange lesions mark its wooden back
and a fruit bowl crustacean clings to its head.

All the light switches have deformed faces,
without eyes or mouth, only a pert nose

continually sneezing, on and off.
The windows are blind and dream days.

Sometimes they weep a million tears
or creak open with a sigh.

The kitchen sink is an alcoholic
who mumbles incoherently about the sea.

It swallows great gulps of *Fairy Liquid*,
singing songs of ocean adventure.

The ceiling is a giant's hand
without fingers or thumbs,

dangling a yoyo light bulb
from the centre of its palm.

Wanderlust

I enter the train toilet to wash
my hands but a plant
commandeers the sink.

It sprouts from the washbasin,
spreading its branches
through the window.

In hot pursuit
of this leafy mystery,
I strip to the waist,

smear my chest with soap
and squeeze through the tiny opening.
A forest flowers on each carriage top,

forming a whipping tail
of loose roots, wagging the train
under bridges and through towns.

Each flower, shrub, and bush
races away breathless,
shaking off the soil that anchors.

Home School

No bookshelves graced the house
where I grew up. Three blood-clot red
medical journals on a coffee table
represented the written word.

Denied more traditional narratives,
I embraced their tales of pancreatic anxiety,
lymphatic love, testicular tragedy,
abdominal desire. Here, heroes

were flayed alive, their organs on show.
One day (eager to uncover the grand design
hidden beneath my own flesh)
I peeled away skin from my fingers.

My blood spurted, splashed in a bowl of water,
each drop— unique as a letter. Lightheaded,
I dreamt of curing my spiritual cancer,
earning my stripes as a metaphorical doctor.

Following the News

There's a metal gate longing in your kiss.
Together we set sail for the couch,
leaking sand and angry scraps of paper.
For untold reasons the slates on our roof
begin to separate and float away,
taking with them a rubber ball lost years before.

They circle the house once before joining
a shiny slate cyclone devouring the street.
My neighbour looks on from his garden,
a broken slate in each hand,
his own roof not long departed.

'Do something!' You say, turning over in your sleep.
I pluck out my eyes and toss them on the fire.
One million chimney lives go up in smoke
leaving behind a whisper, a neatly written letter,
a wild horse, a blood scream.

The Bank Clerk

A working man's life
is misery. The drudgery.
The monotony. The routine.

Ask T.S. Eliot,
poor ailing bank clerk,
and you'll find an army of undead

treading a path each morning
to gainful employment. First
it broke his health and then

his reason. His wife at home
pining for his poetry, losing her body
to Bertrand Russell! And all for what?

A living wage to salt a thousand
invisible wounds. Ezra Pound
putting his pen through the first 54 lines

of *The Waste Land*, found its true beginning:
'April is the cruellest month'.
Perhaps, he knew better than Eliot

the stark veracity of April, when lilacs mix
with memory and desire, and spring rain
stirs dreamers from their dream.

Rehearsals

standing in doorways   backs to me
craning necks   watching the final unfolding

your doctor crawls through them like a spider
extends a blue gloved hand   red with blood

I shake it   his eyes tear up   music swells
I prepare my great surprise   violins preen   he fluffs his lines

we begin again   this time he claps my naked shoulder
leaving an angry red sun   *how am I   am I sleeping*

who am I sleeping with   I jump the gun   weeping
sobbing into my naked hands   we begin again

this time he appears from beneath feet
more extras   people I don't know   people I haven't met

like a lizard he won't approach me   beckoning impatiently
as though I'm late   holding everything up

I move to him   without speaking
he places an arm around my naked waist

pushes me through the crowd   everyone's taller
corduroy jackets press my face

rough against my naked eyes
whisperings   *it's for the best*

these things are part of life
I approach your bed   ready for my close-up

eager to deliver my lines   we're bathed in holy light
a merciless radiance   exposing confused white sheets

sharpening steel rails bracing your bed
you turn to the window   your lips peeled

your jaw stretched   you appear translucent
unspooling   diaphanous   I miss my cue

clapperboards snap like bones
cameras whirl   unblinking   with eyes like lakes

Respite

I make the trek to the village,
pressing my boots

through snow as though my whole
unexplored life lies ahead. The road

has vanished, buried beneath
something alive with brightness

and celebrating an absence of colour.
Guessing at the centre, I remake the road

in my image, lining it with even footfalls.
I've woken from deep hibernation,

a dull sleep mindless as parades.
The good life awaits somewhere ahead

or hides inside greying hedgerows
melting under buttery streetlamps.

Although dusk's pallor warns of worse
weather to come, insisting this stillness

is merely a temporary truce,
a moment of respite

allowing wreckage to be cleared,
and casualties laid to rest.

Celebration
for Caoimhe Muldoon

The air was still,
I heard a pigeon flap her wings.

It was a soft sound,
like wet towels slapping warm stone.

She appeared to celebrate her flight,
working to rise up to a certain height

and then falling,
surprised, perhaps, by the absence of a breeze.

She circled me in this manner
until I rose to join her.

Caving at Kilcorney

Touch the damp walls
and you'll find a cold,
breathless deliverance,
the stone run smooth by centuries

of underground springs.
Here, silence contemplates
its sanctity, nothing can break
its concentration or disturb

its hypnotic reverie,
each heightened heartbeat
translates as trespass.
This place won't recognise

my busy life or acknowledge
its significance. Here, my failures
are not important failures,
my triumphs absurd.

Monks sought out these caves,
crawled on their knees
as deep as they dared.
Their desire to be silent,

their understanding
of the absolute need for it,
irradiates these caves with lives lived
within sight of the holy.

Play Date

Among the thorns and briars, they built a fairy house.
Things long discarded and left for dead
were dug up and put to good use. Bottle caps
became stepping stones; matchboxes, tables and chairs;

an old rope, a swing, and a sardine can
made an inviting paddling pool.
The fairy house and garden complete,
they rolled up their sleeves and built an altar.

A gnarled tree stump with a flat head was dragged
from the shadows and buried within a ring
of wild flowers. They set a plank before it,
an ancient pew for their invisible congregation.

I called to them, my strange adult voice
reaching over a whispering chasm of twilight,
the souls of my fairy children shrouded in nature,
inventing a new religion before my weary eyes.

Secret Poets

Like a symphony
of secret poets
they convened,
nesting on a masterpiece
of spider web branches.

Ashen clouds,
bark and feather,
each perfect.
Synapse hopping to and fro
like the birth
of some beautiful thought.

With a climax,
beyond me,
they rise.
They send the air spinning,
leaving the tree to mourn
the loss of such life.

The Beacon

Then one day the televisions died or committed suicide,
nobody is sure which. One by one, they winked out,
leaving square fathomless voids in every living room.
Old women fiddled with aerials. Old men banged
their fists on hard plastic. Children pressed themselves
against cold screens, disappearing and reappearing
through their dark reflections.

Laptops, tablets, and phones went next,
forgetting themselves and their function.
A farmer from Roscommon proclaimed
this catastrophe signalled the end of the world.
Everyone else suspected terrorism,
then suspected each other, then grew sick
and tired of suspecting everyone and everything,
and so went to bed early and made love.

Weeks passed and skips grew fat with discarded
technology – belching hard drives and vomiting cables.
A conceptual artist based in Thurles received
an Arts Council grant and immediately settled
an outstanding debt owed to his bookie. With the balance,
he collected every last computer, keyboard and screen.
He rolled up his sleeves and set to work,
erecting a monumental totem on Dun Laoghaire Pier.

At first, he titled the work, TOWER OF BABEL!
But following a community meeting (involving

a hard-core element of the local yacht club),
he renamed the piece, The Beacon.
They lit a fire on its highest point
and everyone seemed quite pleased with it.

Although a local politician labelled it 'an eyesore'
in the hope of garnering a few extra votes.
But he misjudged the mood of the people and lost his seat.
'The Beacon can be seen from Holyhead,' people said.
And indeed, it was true. On a clear day, anyone
out for a stroll on Holyhead beach could clearly discern
The Beacon, its message, this shrine to our past.

Lost & Found

I find him, the metal detectorist,
sweeping the beach at dawn.
A pendulum arm swinging, he uncovers
bottle caps and mottled tin cans.
These, he tosses aside, out of his path,
never looking where they land.

I follow their clink and glint
to an unexpected flash of home,
those heavy-curtained rooms determined
to catch and hold my surprise returning.

Thin veils of dust coat mirrors,
dampening reflections. This is how illness grows,
spreading through wide-open plains
to settle in tight corners.

I find him again, digging with his foot –
a stork clearing out its nest. He kneels
and plants his fists in pale-faced stone.
Finding a key, he unlocks the tide
and escapes alone.

Prayer

Is there anything as tragic
as an unfinished poem?

That cul-de-sac where words and inspiration
fail. All those beginnings and lost endings,

I'll pray for. Given a chance, oh how I'd
gather you up in my arms, comfort you,

ease your suffering. I'd become
the ending you seek and release

you into conclusion. So, come to me,
your first letter is enough,

that initial flourish, a fencer's salute,
a hand reaching out in the dark.

Emily

She paces narrow dimensions,
dressed in white,
unpicking the stitches
that secure the floor to the ceiling.

Always turning away from the door,
she opens a window and quickly retreats.
The voice of God echoes through the garden.
It calls to her constantly. If she answers,
she'll slip through a crack in the day.

The desk coaxes her to its side
and consoles her with garlands
of order and purpose.
It gains her confidence
only to betray her
in matters of deepest consequence.

Exhausted, she undresses,
falling into an empty bed.
Her desire ignites and scatters sparks
across icy sheets. They smooth her flat
as personal revelation and neatly
fold her out of consciousness.

Lohan

Out the back garden,
in a gap between the coal bunker
and trampoline, I practise Tai Chi.

Bemused, the cat looks on
as I strum harps of pure energy,
embrace positively charged ions,

and invert the moon.
I remember to breathe
and visualise the Lohan outside his temple —

impervious to the seasons,
rain running down his face.
He looks deep within,

consumed by an immensity of peace,
a slight smile tells us, he has 'made it',
he has found the essential element,

but then, refused to grasp it.
To know what matters and what does not
is the lesson that we long to be taught.

Pawing my holiday brochures,
the cat dreams of a package getaway
to some discounted corner of the cosmos.

I Found the Words

I found the words scattered on the lawn:

WEDDING FIRE CHILD

They stood out in black
against a white background, printed
on miniature placards.
I gathered all I could carry
and laid them out on my desk.
Some immediately pulled together,
hitching up like tractor and trailer:

BLUEBELLS HARDWOOD CLOCKWORK

Some tickled me pink:

BANANA WOOLY GOGGLES

Others pushed their way doggedly
into my hand, bluntly demanding something:

FAITH VIOLENCE JUSTICE

I sorted them as best I could, creating
pretty towers of well-balanced metre.
Although over time, my passion for them failed.
No construct ever went far enough,
everything became mere birdsong.

At my wits' end,
I bunched them into a verbose bouquet
and tossed them from my window.
They fluttered away, coming together
and drifting apart, singing my great failure
upon a sympathetic summer breeze.

The Singing Scab

The scab on my shin
Has started singing
First thing
Each morning
It wakes me with an aria
I tried picking it
But my fingernail refused to get involved
So I've been reduced
To earplugs
And watching the calendar
Waiting for the day
It will dry up
And fall off
I hear it now
Belting out *Vicci d'arte*
How will I survive another encore
My traitor foot
Tapping along
My rebel spirit
Soaring
My poor baton heart
Helpless as an undertaker
Keeping time and pouring tea

The Tuesday I spied a man discovering his soul

Last Tuesday,
from the corner of my eye,
I spied a man discovering his soul.

He sat quietly by himself,
swallowed by his overcoat,
buried in his newspaper
when, to our mutual astonishment,
he found a long coarse hair
growing from the centre of his palm.

A moment of intense confusion followed.
He looked frantically about
and I pretended to be a tourist.
Realising no help was forthcoming,
he heroically recovered his wits
and violently tugged at it.

Imagine his face
as the hair came free
bringing with it
a long colourful feather
that appeared to be the root.

Graveyard Mass

We, the living, hover still as hawks
above the earth-disturbed confines of the dead.
Hearts clutched full of diamond memory,
we summon the deceased from their rest.

They stumble from their graves,
blind, devoid of reason,
reaching out for our impossible embrace.
Silenced by loss, regret,
the unsaid, the unknowable,
we swing them high toward the belfry.

Beneath a surgical white canopy
the priest neatly opens and closes
our wounds, hushing the living and dead
back to sleep with a final, Amen.

Casting Off

Cliffs find themselves again
and again behind stone walls
the same colour as the sea.
My tiny sailboat secured bodily

to the waves breathes its ups
and downs. Pushing harbour hard,
I seek open water, leaving behind
burnt gorse and scorched beaches.

I remember old documentaries,
grainy footage of lava encountering
the ocean, the steaming hiss,
the defiant fire unstoppable, unquenchable.

I press my oars through something
which resists and gives way.
Seagulls cry out and give up their chase.
Nothing can follow me here.

Musical Chairs

Music— loud and persistent,
and chairs seeming to move
as children move around them.
A brief silence, then screams,
then children pushing to a chair,
to shelter from the storm.

I stand at the sharp edge of the activity,
seeking her out with small movements
of my head and eyes,
selecting and discarding each child
until I find her, there— seated,
her hands folded neatly in her lap.
Safe.

A small girl is ejected from the game.
With tears and squeals
she races to find her parents.
Finding no one, she stands with a hand
pressed to her eyes, another to her chest.

I move to a door waiting only for me,
but like Lot's wife, I turn on the threshold.
They're spinning again, the ballroom crying out
for those who won't be there when the music stops.

Crossing

I see them sinking beneath our blue ocean,
quiet now, their eyes wide with surprise
as though death appeared in a form
they hadn't expected.

One still clings to a bag
but I see its soft head rupture
and release a carefully packed cargo —
a pair of denim jeans unfurl, a shoe
races back toward the sunlight.

Another turns full circle,
her hair fanning a constant stream of tiny bubbles.
Upside down photographs mock the tragedy,
civilised family portraits smiling upon a world
where young lungs could never inflate with sea water.

Scattered among the human debris,
colourful life jackets catch my eye.
They hover like birds of prey,
invisible beaks sharp as any balance sheet.

A tsunami will wash their faces clean,
scattering purified remains across pristine beaches.

After Surgery

The hospital lamp throws dawn
in two directions – high and low.

Its fantail of light reaches so far
before losing its way in the dark.

A rich emptiness sends its heralds
racing through my body,

its banners whipping my skin,
its trumpets rattling my bones,

like spoons in a teacup.
When the lamp goes out

darkness blinds
with its feathered edge.

And outside,
a deeper tenebrosity looms,

an unanchored vastness
adrift with meaningless precision.

The Hare

While my wife and child sleep, I creep
downstairs to find the dawn awaiting me.
It softens my garden, dims
impatient greens and celebrates
the beauty to be found in what is grey.

The washing line smiles from branches,
as though amused by a restless mind,
this clacking mill that keeps on grinding.
Then I see her, standing on hind legs,
her antennae ears at full stretch,
her large marble eyes raised,
not in appreciation or praise,
but perfectly free from thought, a directed stillness,
lost to everything, but the astonishing moment.

In this state of ecstasy, a kind of martyrdom,
her rapture receives rather than acts.
Quick as a sigh, she's gone,
disappeared into what is not for my seeking.

The Crucified Christ

My daughter takes in the scene as though,
walking home from school one bright spring morning,
she turned a corner and stumbled upon the crucifixion.

The image holds her, her small face upturned,
unable to look away, her mouth twisted, her eyes wide.

I want to throw a coloured sheet over the iconography
or transform the scene with my words, paint it
again with flowers and castles and heroes.

But this is where we must stand,
at the foot of the cross,
mumbling magic that can never heal a wound.
Our need conjuring the wood and nails,
the unnameable grief and horror. Our pressed hands,
sharp as spears, flying back through time
to pierce his sacred heart.

Grace

The knowing half-light of twilight—
half grief, half enchantment—

streams down on this Apple Green,
this petrol station I enter

in a state of grace. So long
holed up, nursing wounds,

nestled in morphine's velvet embrace.
I dream my way to a cushioned seat.

I find coffee-eyed couples
prodding their phones,

hatching uncertain futures.
I too am hatching,

breaking through. Like a new-born chick,
I fight my way into the world.

You comb grey hair from my eyes,
and it settles, between renewal and decay.

The Bell-Ringers

Taking hold of the sally
with knowledgeable hands,
feet apart,
facing inward,
circled and focused,
they prepare to conjure a storm of iron.
Their arms pull and the rope drops,
racing to the bottom of silence.

Silver tongued tulips
toss their heads and bellow thunder,
cornered dust jumps and glitters.
Beneath the bell-ringers' heave,
stained glass saints rattle their frames.

Oh to be circled there,
gripping time by the throat,
lassoing and taming its final secret.
Starved of context,
I can only wrench upon these words,
waiting patiently as a lightning rod
for Arcadia to arrive and strike this page.

A Still Life

Toward the end,
bent like a swan's neck
over his easel,
Manet painted simple flowers.
I can only imagine
the comfort these brought him
during those pain-filled days.

In a crystal vase, his *White Lilac*
has no function except to exist.
Here the lilacs hang like clouds
ablaze with ineffable softness.
Their singleness of being
hovers behind, within, and before,
a block of drabness suspended in time,
and void of light.

Acknowledgements

Acknowledgements are due to the editors of the following where some of these poems appeared for the first time: *Poetry Ireland Review, Cyphers, Irish Times, Sunday Independent, Banshee Press, Strokestown Poetry Anthology, The Blue Nib, Best of Vine Leaves Literary Journal, Dedalus Press (Anthology, Local Wonders), The Sea (Anthology, Rebel Poetry), fathers and what must be said (Anthology, Rebel Poetry), Pandemic.ie, Sixteen Magazine, The Universe Inside (Anthology, Poehemian Press), Poeming Pigeons (Anthology, The Poetry Box), Miracle, Poems of Adventure (Anthology, edited by Jessica Clark and Stephanie Hanson), Kilkenny People, Poetry Ireland (A Bowl of Mysteries).*

My thanks to Ciaran Carty, Derek Coyle, Jane Daly, the Irish Theatre Institute, Arts Council of Ireland, Peggy Ramsey Foundation and Poetry Ireland.

Finally, a special thank you to my wife, Margaret, for all her love and support.

About the Author

Darren is a poet and playwright living in Goresbridge, Co. Kilkenny. His poetry is widely published and in 2020, he received the Dennis O'Driscoll Literary Award. He was writer-in-residence at Carlow College, St Patrick's, 2019, and the 2020 writer-in-residence at the Science Gallery, Trinity College, Dublin.

As a playwright, Darren has worked extensively with the Abbey Theatre. His plays are produced internationally with Irish Repertory Theatre (New York), the Keegan Theatre (Washington DC) Piccolo Teatro (Milan) and Bread and Roses Theatre (London).

His plays garnered a number of awards including the Bread & Roses Playwriting Award, & the Radius Playwriting Prize, in association with Finborough Theatre.

Darren's writing interests are represented by Camila Young at Curtis Brown.

Follow Darren on Twitter at https://twitter.com/DarrenDonohue1
Website: https://donohuegoresbridge.wixsite.com/darren-donohue
Agent: https://www.curtisbrown.co.uk/client/darren-donohue